WA 11625171

Britain in Decline

D0185402

Also by Andrew Gamble

From Alienation to Surplus Value (with Paul Walton)
The Conservative Nation
Capitalism in Crisis (with Paul Walton)
An Introduction to Modern Social and Political Thought
The British Party System and Economic Policy 1945–83
    (with Stuart Walkland)
The Free Economy and the Strong State
Developments in British Politics 4 (co-editor)

Britain in Decline

Economic Policy, Political Strategy and the British State

FOURTH EDITION

Andrew Gamble

© Andrew Gamble 1981, 1985, 1990, 1994

All rights reserved. No reproduction, copy or transmission of this publication may be made without written permission.

No paragraph of this publication may be reproduced, copied or transmitted save with written permission or in accordance with the provisions of the Copyright, Designs and Patents Act 1988, or under the terms of any licence permitting limited copying issued by the Copyright Licensing Agency, 90 Tottenham Court Road, London W1P 9HE.

Any person who does any unauthorised act in relation to this publication may be liable to criminal prosecution and civil claims for damages.

First published 1981
Reprinted twice
Second edition 1985
Reprinted three times
Third edition 1990
Reprinted three times
Fourth edition 1994

Published by
MACMILLAN PRESS LTD
Houndmills, Basingstoke, Hampshire RG21 6XS
and London
Companies and representatives
throughout the world

ISBN 0–333–61440–2 hardcover
ISBN 0–333–61441–0 paperback

A catalogue record for this book is available from the British Library.

10   9   8   7   6   5 . 4   3   2
03   02   01   00   99   98   97   96

Printed in Hong Kong

1162517 1

Learning Resources
Centre

In memory of A. N. Silver

The purely British causes of the economic depression are complex, but they can be summed up in a single sentence. English manufacturing costs are among the highest in the world. If this situation continues, any economic structure based on exports is faced with inevitable ruin . . . England is trying to compete in international markets, and at the same time provide her people with a wage level and a standard of living which does not permit costs to be low enough either to export profitably, or to attract the capital necessary for the development and upkeep of her manufacturing.

André Siegfried, *England's Crisis* (1931)

What with our sentimentality, our Party system, our government by committee, our 'Mandarins', our 'Society', and our Generals . . . the game is just hopeless . . . Our political organisation is thoroughly rotten, almost non-existent. It is Carthaginian – really the only comparison I can think of. Never was there such an absurd waste of power, such ridiculous inconsequence of policy – not for want of men but for want of any effective central authority or dominant idea to make them work together.

Lord Milner (1909)

Shame is a kind of anger turned in on itself. And if a whole nation were to feel ashamed it would be like a lion recoiling in order to spring. I admit that even this shame is not yet to be found in Germany; on the contrary the wretches are still patriots. But if the ridiculous system of our new knight does not disabuse them of their patriotism, then what will? . . . The state is too serious a business to be subjected to such buffoonery. A Ship of Fools can perhaps be allowed to drift before the wind for a good while; but it will still drift to its doom precisely because the fools refuse to believe it possible. This doom is the approaching revolution.

Karl Marx (1843)

Contents

vii

Acknowledgements

The author and publishers wish to thank the following who have kindly given permission for the use of copyright material: Banco Nazionale Del Lavoro for data from an article 'Phases of Capitalist Development' by A. Maddison, published in the June 1977 issue of the Bank's *Quarterly Review*; The Controller of Her Majesty's Stationery Office for data from Royal Commission on Trade Unions and Employers' Associations, *Report* and *Employment Gazette*; National Institute of Economic and Social Research for tables from *Review*; Organisation for Economic Co-operation and Development for tables from OECD Reports, National Accounts 1961–7 and *Economic Outlook*, July 1979 and June 1993.

Preface

This book was a product of the 1970s and first appeared in 1981 at the beginning of the great economic and political shakeout which accompanied the Thatcher Government's attempt to reverse British decline. The second and third editions were prepared and appeared during the Thatcher era. This fourth edition has been prepared after its end. Much has changed since the book was first written, and my perspective on many of the issues discussed in these pages has changed also. In all the later editions, however, I have kept changes to the main chapters to a minimum, leaving them as a commentary on the debates and the solutions proposed in the 1970s. The main changes over the four editions have been to the Introduction, to Chapter 1 and to the Conclusion. The final chapter has been completely rewritten, and in this fourth edition offers an assessment of the achievements and the significance of the Thatcher Government in the context of the long debate on British decline.

The original title of the book was *The Politics of Decline*, which in certain respects expresses more accurately the contents and approach of the book. It is a study of how decline has been perceived and the perceptions of decline and of the political struggles to reverse decline, rather than of decline as an external objective process. Whether there has been a decline and whether it can be measured depends on whether there is such an entity as the British national economy. In the era of national protectionism in the world economy which has now ended, the British political elite certainly believed there was such an entity, and perceived Britain to be in decline both as a world power and as a national economy. It is this perception and the historical experience which informs it which is the main subject of this book.

Many people helped me write it. I owe a great deal to

students at Sheffield who attended my course on political economy. I also learnt much from discussion with friends and colleagues and I would particularly like to thank Jerry Agnew, Anthony Arblaster, David Baker, Peter Duff, Brian Duncan, Stephen George, Ankie Hoogvelt, Eddie Jachcel, Steve Ludlam, David Marquand, Bryan Mason, Tony Payne, Ben Rosamond, Quentin Rudland, Patrick Seyd, Martin Smith, Ian Taylor and Stuart Walkland.

My wider intellectual debts are too many to mention. They are apparent on every page of this book. Its judgements and arguments lean heavily on the work of others. This book would not have been possible without the pioneering work of Perry Anderson and Tom Nairn in their seminal essay in *New Left Review* in the 1960s which opened up a new range of questions about the interpretation of English history. Henry Drucker, Martin Jacques and Ralph Miliband encouraged me to develop in essay form some of the ideas explored in this book. Henk Overbeek and Bob Jessop, through their writings on decline, stimulated me to clarify some of my conceptions, as, did two conferences organised by Michael Mann in Cambridge in 1988 and Uffe Ostergaard in Aarhus in 1991.

The book was nursed into life by four Macmillan editors: Shaie Selzer, Rob Shreeve, John Winckler and Steven Kennedy. I owe a great deal in particular to Steven Kennedy for his special and much appreciated assistance and advice. Thanks are also due to Keith Povey, who has been an extremely efficient and helpful copy-editor for all four editions; and to Hazel Watson, who prepared the original typescript. My family gave me great support throughout the writing of this book, as did Neil Lyndon, even if it turned out rather differently from what he expected.

I owe a special debt to Yoshi Ogasawara, who studied with me in Sheffield and undertook the laborious task of translating the book into Japanese. The Japanese take a special interest in the question of Britain's decline, perhaps in the spirit of Marx's advice to the Germans that they heed the lessons of British development – 'De Te Fabula Narratur.'

Sheffield
November 1993

Andrew Gamble

Introduction

It is remarkable to see how relatively numerous in declining empires are the people capable of making the right diagnosis and preaching some sensible cure. It is no less remarkable, however, that wise utterances generally remain sterile, because, as Gonzales de Cellorigo forcefully put it while watching impotently the decline of Spain, 'those who can will not and those who will cannot'.

Carlo Cipolla[1]

Britain has now been in decline for a hundred years. It has become the most observed and analysed decline in modern history, provoking a speculative literature of enormous dimensions. Few explanations have not been proffered, few causes not dissected, few remedies not canvassed at least twice. The decline has been the central fact about British politics for a century, a major preoccupation of its public intellectuals and intermittently but increasingly of its political leaders. Two processes stand out – the absolute decline in the power and status of the British imperial state, and the relative decline of the British economy with its long-standing failure to match the rates of expansion of its rivals.

The starting point of Britain's decline was the position of unrivalled dominance it had achieved during the nineteenth century. By 1900 Britain controlled over one-fifth of the world's land surface and ruled one-quarter of the world's population. Its land forces remained small but its navy was still maintained at a level where it would be superior to the two next most powerful navies combined. The foundations of this empire had been the commercial and strategic policies pursued by the British state for 250 years. Its consolidation and further extension in the nineteenth century had been the result of the industrial and technological lead Britain established by being the first major economy to industrialise. The height of Britain's industrial domination of the world was reached in the middle decades of the nineteenth century. At that time one third of the world's output of manufactured goods came from Britain. Britain produced half the world's coal and iron, half the world's cotton goods, almost half its steel. From this position Britain conducted one-quarter of the world's trade and built up a massive commercial and financial predominance. Even in 1900 Britain still accounted for one-third of the world's exports of manufactures, and the registered tonnage of British shipping was more than the tonnage of the rest of the world combined. London was the unchallenged commercial and financial centre of the new capitalist world economy. The international monetary system was centred upon the gold standard and the pound sterling, and British foreign investments had risen by 1914 to the remarkable total of £4000 million.

By the last decade of the twentieth century a very different picture presented itself. The British Empire had disappeared. Only a few last outposts such as Hong Kong and the Falkland Islands remained. Britain retained some of the trappings of a great power. It still had a nuclear arsenal, substantial and well-equipped armed forces, and a permanent seat on the UN Security Council. But it was no longer the kind of global power it had been in the first half of the century, and its proud tradition of sovereign independence was increasingly circumscribed by the new realities and requirements of interdependence. The security and economic relationships forged with the United States and Western Europe after 1945 were indications of how limited British sovereignty had become.

The British economy was incomparably richer and more productive in 1990 than in 1900 but it was no longer the world leader or the powerhouse of the world economy. It remained one of the richest economies in the world, but its position and performance relative to other economies in the leading group had substantially weakened. On a range of indicators Britain had slipped behind and despite several determined attempts showed no signs of being able to catch up.

The slope of Britain's descent has not been constant. There

have been periods of recovery, even of advance and success, but they do not affect the overall judgement that Britain in the twentieth century has been a state in decline and that the efforts of its governing class have failed to arrest that decline. The problems surrounding Britain's future have accumulated while the reserves for meeting them have dwindled.

There is a vast literature on decline but little agreement about how decline should be defined and still less about how it should be explained. This is hardly surprising. Decline is to an important extent a matter of political perception rather than an objective reality. To study decline is to study the perceptions and responses of the British governing class during the last hundred years. For many of them the decline in world power and the relative decline in economic performance are inextricably linked. They are part of the same process.

The crucial contexts which have shaped the domestic debates on decline and what to do about it have been formed by Britain's changing place in the world order. There have been three key debates, which are examined in this book – the debate on National Efficiency before 1914; the debate on modernisation from the 1920s through to the 1960s; and the debate on social democracy from the 1960s through to the present. These debates succeed one another chronologically, although they also overlap, and arguments and positions from the earlier debates often reappear in the later ones.

One of the most persistent aspects of the discourse on decline is the belief in a 'British disease', a malady whose causes lie deep in British psychology and British culture. A popular diagnosis of this 'disease' in the 1960s and 1970s was that the country was living beyond its means. The British consumed too much and worked too little. As one Labour minister memorably put it: 'For generations this country has not earned an honest living'.[2]

What made such assertions plausible were repeated economic crises – over the balance of payments,[3] public expenditure, and pay. The nation it was said was importing more than it exported, the government was spending more than it raised in taxes, and the workers were demanding the distribution of a bigger cake than the one they were producing. The consequences of such behaviour was placing Britain's future prosperity and its traditional freedoms in danger.

The favourite political scapegoat for the British disease used to be the trade unions. Their behaviour was most frequently cited as the reason why Britain's payments would not balance, why public expenditure was out of control and was beginning to encroach on 'our plural society',[4] and why inflation was accelerating.[5] Sir Keith Joseph summed up twenty years of anti-union criticism in the title of a speech delivered in 1979 during the Winter of Discontent: 'Solving the trade union problem is the key to Britain's economic recovery.'[6]

When Margaret Thatcher left office in 1990 trade unions had been weakened by a decade of high unemployment and anti-union legislation. The Government claimed the change in the climate of industrial relations as one of their greatest successes. Management had regained the power to manage. But the symptoms of the British disease appeared little affected. The public finances and the balance of payments were once again out of control and heading for record deficits. Inflation was rising sharply and the economy was moving back into recession. Solving the trade union problem, it seems, was not enough.

Many writers on decline had never thought it was. Some have attempted to explain Britain's post-war failure in terms of the cyclical patterns at work in the history of all great empires. Parallels for Britain's experience have been sought in the declines of other great imperial powers – Rome, Venice, Spain. As in other small states which have created empires the qualities and attitudes which assisted Britain to rise and expand were discarded or neglected by the later generations which inherited the imperial position. They developed instead tastes, needs, and activities which were sustainable only so long as Britain retained its economic and military leadership, yet which tended to undermine the basis of that strength. Britain's rise to world power was followed by the development of a pervasive 'anti-enterprise' culture and a social conservatism at all levels, particularly in education and business management, which persistently blocked successful modernisation and adaptation.

Trade unions are part of this 'anti-enterprise culture' but
not the only or the most important part. The real source of
Britain's decline is traced to the attitudes and the behaviour of
political elites.[7] Such is the argument of two of the most
influential books published on British decline in recent years –
Corelli Barnett's *The Audit of War* and Martin Wiener's *English
Culture and the Decline of the Industrial Spirit, 1870–1980*. Both
were cited by Thatcherite ministers as evidence that Britain
required a radical change in the climate of ideas, a cultural
revolution, to rebuild a vibrant capitalist economy.

Barnett argued in his study of the shortcomings of British
industry in the second world war that the problems of poor
management, overmanning, restrictive practices, low investment, and low productivity were rife throughout British
industry even during the war-time economy, which according
to official accounts had been one time when the British
economy had performed well. Barnett argued that the
euphoria of victory allowed these failings to be ignored.
Postwar reconstruction was fatally flawed by being directed
on the one hand to the building of a universal welfare state, a
New Jerusalem, a project which had come to dominate the
thinking of the bulk of the British political elite, and on the
other hand to the preservation of Britain's world role. Both
New Jerusalem and the world role assumed a strong economy
which no longer existed. Their spending programmes were
therefore erected on very shaky foundations.

Critics of this cultural or 'declinist' thesis have argued that
the evidence for it is highly selective; that the whole notion of
decline is an illusion; and that it has often been used as a way
of justifying technocratic and authoritarian policy solutions.[8]
The standpoint of this book is rather different. The cultural
thesis often presents an exaggerated and misleading picture of
the British economy and its performance, but its critics are
sometimes in danger of asserting the contrary – that there has
been no decline at all, and that all the problems dealt with as
problems of decline are no more than normal problems of
change and adjustment. This book analyses decline in two
main ways: first as a discourse which was constituted by the
particular ideas and assumptions of those participating in it;
secondly as a historical process, a set of circumstances and

constraints which defined the limits within which the debate proceeded.

Understanding British decline as a historical process requires analysis of the complex interplay between the decline in British power and the decline in British competitiveness. What was different about Britain's Empire compared with the great empires of the past was that it became inextricably linked with a global process of capital accumulation which resulted in the creation of an interdependent world economy and a rate of growth of population and material wealth far surpassing any levels previously achieved in human history.[9]

Britain's expansion may have been launched upon foundations that were similar to those of many previous empires, but it reached its zenith and was consolidated under very different ones. When earlier empires that arose from a self-sufficient agricultural base collapsed, the imperial state was forced back to this base, once decline had reached a certain point. That possibility disappeared for Britain during the nineteenth century. At a certain stage of its development Britain abandoned such foundations, merging its future irrevocably with the wider world economy.

All discussion of British decline must start from Britain's relationship to the world economy that was the means of Britain's rise, which was transformed in the course of that rise, and to which Britain remains tied. What has to be explained is why the most dynamic and expansionist nation in modern European history, the organiser of the largest world empire, the pioneer of industrialisation, and the country renowned above all others for continuity of its institutions and the political skill of its ruling class, should have lost out during the last thirty years in competition with Germany, France, and Japan. The eclipse of British military power by the United States and Russia was widely forecast as early as the 1840s because of the much greater human and physical resources they could command. What was not anticipated was the relative inability of the British *economy* to maintain its dynamism and compete with its rivals.

A central problem for British historiography in the twentieth century has been why the British economy proved so weak and why political attempts to overcome this weakness were not successful. The unevenness of the development of different economies and regions within the world economy has been a noted feature of the modern era. Recognition of backwardness has acted as a spur for states to modernise themselves and catch up with the economic leaders. According to this argument the disappearance of Britain's lead over its competitors was entirely predictable. What is not so easily explained is the feebleness of the British response. Charles Feinstein has argued that 'the leader who falls behind will ultimately respond to the changed circumstances and in particular to the increased threat to markets and jobs created by the formerly backward economies.'[10] Yet although Britain had clearly lost its economic leadership to the United States by 1914, and had fallen behind other competitors in the 1950s and 1960s the response was a very long time in coming.

One explanation is that for most of the period of its decline the British state has proved able to negotiate a gradual descent. At no point did failing power threaten a major rupture in institutional continuity or an irreversible collapse of British prosperity. The decline in the world power of the British state occurred in stages. The continuing expansion of the British economy helped to compensate for that decline and to limit its impact. The British state used its considerable political, ideological, economic and financial resources, which had been accumulated during the period of British dominance of the world economy, to buy time, to stave off challenges and to delay adjustments. When crises shook the world economy, the British state and the British economy were strong enough to ride them out. But this success reduced the will to tackle many internal weaknesses which gradually became more significant as Britain's relative position deteriorated.

During the world economic downturn in the 1970s, the relative weakness of the British economy, tolerated for so long, became increasingly unsupportable, and brought growing political and social tensions. The world recession changed the political climate by threatening to turn relative decline into absolute decline. Some observers argued that there was no general crisis of capitalism, only a crisis of capitalism in Britain. But general crises always take the form of national crises, and their impact is uneven depending on the ability of

each state to protect itself, drawing on whatever resources and
strengths it has. The consequences of a recession like the
consequences of a boom are unevenly distributed because the
world economy is an interdependent economic system rather
than a group of self-contained national economies. To analyse
the economic policy of a nation-state like Britain it is
important to place Britain in the context of the wider world
system.

In the 1970s Britain came to be widely perceived as a weak
link among the leading economic powers. The worries about
the balance of payments, inflation, and public spending were
symptoms of wider anxieties about Britain's economic future,
because of the apparently unstoppable tide of imports and the
inability of so many sectors of British industry to compete.
The extent of the shakeout which took place in the 1970s and
1980s prompted many people to ask how much further the
contraction could go. What would be the end of it? A Britain
with no industry at all? Unemployment and destitution of an
unimaginable scale? Exports insufficient even to pay for the
imports needed to feed the population? The fears were not
new. Joseph Chamberlain, Radical, Imperialist, and Tariff
Reformer, declared in 1903:[11]

> Agriculture, as the greatest of all trades and industries of
> this country, has been practically destroyed. Sugar has
> gone; silk has gone; iron is threatened; wool is threatened;
> cotton will go! How long are you going to stand it?

Many found it difficult to comprehend how a nation that
was on the winning side in two world wars could lose the
peace and succumb to the commercial challenge of rivals
defeated on the battlefield. How could a nation that showed
such unity in the Second World War, and was so long
renowned for its traditions of civility and consensus, appear to
disunited and racked by conflict, envy, and cynicism in the
1960s and 1970s? Why was Britain, unable to achieve an
economic miracle in the 1950s, still unable to achieve one in
the 1960s when so many faults had been identified and so
many remedies proposed, and when, for a time, all parties and
all major interests subscribed to growth and a strategy for
modernising the British economy?

What we call decline is a product of political perception and definition. The ways in which it is explained are often not independent of the political remedies proposed to deal with it. This book is about the various ways in which decline has been defined and explained, and the political strategies that have emerged to tackle it. It offers an account of Britain's historical development not as a unique self-contained experience but as the interaction between the external expansion of the state and the internal formation of its principal classes and institutions. Only if Britain is viewed as part of the world economic and political system can the national aspects of British development be properly located. Without a world system perspective the real 'peculiarities' of British development are lost to view.[12]

This book is divided into three parts. Part I explores the concept of decline, examines how it might be measured, and discusses how it has been perceived in the major intellectual debates. Part II discusses the specific historical roots of decline; the history of the British state and the dominant patterns of external expansion and internal compromise; and the history of the working class.

Part III explores three perspectives – market, state, and class – which have dominated debates on decline and which have helped to form political strategies and programmes for overcoming it. Chapter 4 considers the modernisation programmes of the 1960s and 1970s. Chapters 5 and 6 look at the new strategies which emerged in the 1970s in response to the apparent failure of modernisation, the free market strategy of the right and the alternative economic strategy of the left.

The term 'strategy' is here used to mean a discourse on economic policy and political action which is unified and bounded by certain shared assumptions about the desirable relationship between the state and the economy. It identifies long-term objectives and means of achieving them. A strategy in this sense is different from the political programme of a particular party, although it may influence it.

The final chapter assesses whether the Thatcher era is best understood as the long-awaited political response which restructured the economy and brought the decline to an end, or as merely the latest episode in that decline.

PART 1
DECLINE

1

The hundred years' decline

This nation has to be mobilised and rallied for a tremendous effort . . . If that effort is not made we may soon come to crisis, to a real crisis. I do not fear that so much, for this reason, that in a crisis this nation is always at its best. This people knows how to handle a crisis, it cools their heads and steels their nerves. What I fear much more than a sudden crisis is a long, slow, crumbling through the years until we sink to the level of a Spain, a gradual paralysis, beneath which all the vigour and energy of this country will succumb. That is a far more dangerous thing and far more likely to happen unless some effort is made.

Oswald Mosley[1]

To speak of British decline is to isolate a national economy and a state that are British and are declining. But decline should not be confused with decay, nor with a process of internal decomposition. During its rise to world power the British state abandoned self-sufficiency and became dependent for its survival on the wider world economy. British decline is not therefore primarily an internal question of morals and customs, but depends on perceiving the British state and national economy within the world political and economic order, which Britain helped to construct and of which the British economy remains an integral part. Britain's successes and failures are accordingly measured against the successes and failures of other states in the world system, and much of the writing on decline is a deliberate attempt to identify what is peculiar to British experience.

1.1 Britain and the world economy

This world economy into which Britain was integrated has passed through a number of stages in its development. During the long mercantilist period which began in the fifteenth century, a world market arose based upon colonies, sea power and a protected trade in primary commodities and slaves. It was followed in the nineteenth century by a brief era of free trade, which was made possible by the development of capitalist industry in Britain. It encouraged a division of labour between different parts of the world economy based on the exchange of manufactured goods for primary products. Britain exploited its advantage as the first industrial nation to the full by throwing open its markets and attempting to persuade or force all other states to do the same. Agriculture was sacrificed for the greater gains that flowed from specialising in manufactures. The history of the world economy was increasingly determined by the worldwide accumulation of capital. This involved a progressive widening and deepening of the world division of labour. The world market embraced more and more countries and the pressures of competitive accumulation enforced ever greater degrees of specialisation and ever greater interdependence of production. The emergence of this new world economy is the major historical event of modern times.

The free-trade period was succeeded by a national protectionist period after 1880, marked by intense commercial and strategic rivalry between the great powers, strong pressures towards the formation of blocs, and two world wars. After 1945 the world economy was split into two major competing blocs which enjoyed considerable internal unity. The capitalist bloc was unified under American leadership and competition between national economies and nation-states receded as the leading sectors of industry began to be organised transnationally and pressures developed for the convertibility of currencies and the reduction of tariff barriers. A further development of the division of labour became evident in the new pattern of trade which emerged. Trade between the advanced industrial countries grew fastest during the long post-war boom, and soon became more important than the complementary trade between the producers of manufactures and the producers of food and raw materials.[2] It was evident also in the changing character of the capitalist enterprise. The main agent of capital accumulation in the early industrial revolution had been the businesses based upon small work-shops and single factories. Competitive accumulation had seen these give way in sector after sector, first to multi-divisional and multi-product national firms, and then to international companies. These now operated globally, were highly diversified, and could deploy huge financial and productive resources.[3] Dominating the world economy, they were no longer tied to a single national base. National economies and nation-states still remained, but their import-ance and their independence were qualified by this new interpenetration of the production empires of capital.

With the collapse of communism in eastern Europe and the Soviet Union between 1989 and 1991, and the rapid develop-ment of capitalism in China a new period of development of the world economy has commenced. The world economy has been reunified, and there are strong pressures towards the re-establishment of global free trade and the extension of global finance and global production. At the same time there are pressures towards the formation of regional identities and institutions, particularly in Europe and North America. Both these tendencies are reducing the former scope and importance of the nation-state as a decision-making centre.

British decline both as a historical process and as a political discourse belong to the national protectionist period of world economic development. In the years since 1880 three main phases of decline can be identified, although it is important to recognise that since 'decline' depends upon political perception the 'hundred years decline' means not that there has been a continuous downward trend in British economic performance and military power, but that decline has been a key preoccupation of the political elite for one hundred years.

The first phase of decline understood in this sense was between 1880 and 1914 when Britain first suffered major competition from industrial rivals, and shortcomings in British industry began to be noticed. A major but unsuccessful challenge to the ruling free-trade policy of the British state was mounted by Joseph Chamberlain and the Social Imperialists. The second phase – between the two world wars – saw a much weakened Britain attempting and failing to rebuild its world power, but managing to avoid the worst effects of the world slump of the 1930s. The internal challenge of the Labour movement was contained for the moment, and the lesser challenge of Fascism resisted. In the third phase after 1945 Britain, now subordinate financially and militarily to the United States, and shorn of a substantial part of its accumulated wealth, was forced to withdraw from its empire, and failed to grow or invest at the same rate as other capitalist national economies during the long post-war boom. As a result its position grew steadily more vulnerable.

The period of decline had seen Britain change from a position of world leadership and dominance to one of weakness and dependence, its fortunes increasingly linked to a world economic system over which the British state could exert less and less control. For a long time the seriousness of Britain's position was concealed by the prosperity and buoyancy of the post-war western economy. But with the downturn in the 1970s a new phase opened both in the history of the world economy and in Britain's decline. Britain entered it with heavy burdens and facing daunting tasks.

1.2 The long boom

A major world recession erupted in 1974–5. It marked the decisive end of the longest and most rapid period of continuous expansion world capitalism has ever enjoyed, and opened a period of much more uncertain and uneven economic progress. Because the boom was so prolonged and so general there is a paradox in speaking of British 'decline' since 1945, since in absolute terms the British economy had never been so prosperous, nor had it ever expanded so fast.[4] This boom was unannounced and largely unexpected, but once it was properly under way many came to believe it could be a boom without end. The general downturn that began at the end of 1973 was not widely accepted at first as the turning point it has since been acknowledged to be.[5]

The widespread predictions made after 1945 of an early return to the slow growth, stagnant demand and high unemployment of the 1930s proved false because of major changes which the world war had brought about. It created a new set of investment opportunities, new social relations between capital and labour, and new political relations between the leading capitalist states, which helped to create for almost twenty-five years a most favourable environment for accumulation. These conditions were fortuitous in the sense that no central authority designed them or planned them, although their coming into being had always been possible, since there was never any doubt that there was great scope for a further development of the productive forces under capitalism. Capitalist development has never proceeded smoothly but always unevenly, in great uncontrollable spurts followed by equally uncontrollable periods of slump and stagnation.

As an economic system capitalism has always been marked by instability, which arises principally from its own internal compulsion to expand. Capital accumulation is an immensely powerful mode of production, yet it has become increasingly fragile. It has expanded material wealth far more than any previous mode of production, and has made possible the construction of a world economy that is based not just on trade but upon a world division and specialisation of labour. On both counts it marks a crucial watershed in human history. In its quest for profits capital seeks to overcome all obstacles in the path of its accumulation. That is why competitive capital accumulation between individual enter-prises has no resting place short of the complete automation of the production process and the industrialisation of the whole world. But its progress towards these limits has been interrupted by great crises of over-production, because the accumulation of capital constantly tends to race ahead of the conditions that can sustain it. Capitalism as a world system has suffered twenty such general crises of over-production since 1825.[6] They have become progressively more severe, because the scale of production and degree of interdependence have grown during every period of expansion.[7]

The great post-war expansion that finally ended in 1973

rested on conditions that released once more the springs of capitalist advance.[8] A wide range of new investment opportunities emerged, particularly in cars, electronics, and construction, which boosted average profitability in a wide band of industrial sectors. There was a plentiful supply of labour, and in many countries, particularly in those which had suffered Fascist rule, labour was weakly organised. There were also many new supplies of labour as yet untapped in agriculture, amongst women, and in less developed regions of the world economy, and there were abundant and cheap supplies of energy and raw materials. Political regimes were now quite ready to extend government involvement in the economy and to remove many costs and insecurities from the shoulders of individual enterprises.[9]

But there was another condition which was crucial. Despite the fact that capitalism was a world economic system with a tendency to expand to its limit, the world economy has always been fragmented by the existence of national economies and nation states. Capital accumulation was still organised within territorial units, and each government claimed sovereignty over its own economy, the right to pursue and support the economic interests of its own industries, and the capacity to maintain the minimal conditions for internal capital accumulation: in particular, a national economic market, effective laws on property, contract and labour, a stable currency, and the ability to raise taxes. Responsibility for maintaining the conditions for the functioning of the world market was accepted by no one. Yet from the beginning the prosperity of capitalist economies depended crucially on the delicate networks of the world economy, its markets and its division of labour, and on the free flow of goods, capital, and labour.[10]

In the history of world capitalism this responsibility has been borne by two states, Britain and the United States, because each for a time was the unchallenged industrial and financial centre of the world economy. The United States after 1945 took over the role Britain had been performing with increasing difficulty, and set out to rebuild the shattered international monetary system and trading network of the capitalist world, as well as to unify it politically and militarily against the Soviet Union. The stability of the western world and the pace of its economic advance owed much to the challenged leadership and domination of the United States which was able as a result to impose its own terms and its own solutions.[11]

The factories which made the boom possible and sustained it eventually became exhausted. The intensive exploitation of the new investment opportunities eventually led to their exhaustion. New technological systems of the same scope which might form the leading sectors of a future expansion were not available. Supplies of cheap labour that are easily or safely available had been used up, and in the advanced western states the working class had become highly organised and highly paid. State expenditure and state involvement in the economy had been pushed to the point where they created a fiscal crisis of expenditures outrunning revenues, and accelerating inflation. Finally, the very success of the United States in creating the conditions in the world economy for the boom led directly to the recovery of rivals, particularly Germany and Japan, and the closing of the productivity gap between them and the United States. The levels of American foreign investment and overseas military spending were only supportable indefinitely so long as the allies of the United States agreed to finance them. Their refusal caused the downfall of the dollar and the eventual disintegration in 1971 of the international monetary system which the Americans had designed and upheld after the war.[12] It signalled the end of a phase of development of world capitalism which the recession in 1974–6 confirmed.

If capitalism is seen as a world system as well as a collection of national economics, the division between the leading group of capitalist states and the rest of the world economy is what is most striking. The relative strengths and weaknesses of the members of the leading group are problems of much smaller magnitude than the gulf between the developed and the underdeveloped. It is important to remember this throughout the discussion in this book. Amidst all the talk of British decline it is sometimes possible to forget that Britain remains one of the wealthiest countries in the world.

When Britain is placed in the context of the world economy, its apparently peculiar and special problems often lose their

uniqueness and are seen to be problems shared by all the
leading capitalist states. Periods of boom and periods of
recessions affect all economies. So do changes in prices of
primary commodities and energy. There are significant
differences between states, but these arise within a context of
common institutions and common structures, such as the
increasing scale of industrial enterprises; the application of
science to production; the widening of the market to embrace
all occupations, social groups and nations; the great expansion
of the state; the growth of trade unions and the establishment
of mass democracy. These have generated many common
problems, of which the most important in recent years has
been to find ways to fund state expenditures, which have risen
inexorably and apparently irreversibly in every state, and at
the same time to contain the inflation which has become since
the war a permanent feature of western capitalist economies.[13]
The key to both has long been seen as engineering a faster rate
of growth, because it effortlessly generates higher tax revenues
and permits demands to be more easily reconciled with
resources at lower levels of inflation. But it is precisely growth
that can no longer be relied upon or stimulated in the old
ways. In the 1970s Britain's leisurely relative decline in
economic performance threatened to turn into something
potentially much more serious.

1.3 The measurement of decline

British decline can only be understood, and in some sense only
perceived, when it is related to the world economy which
Britain once dominated and to which it has remained chained
long after its dominance has passed away. The British have
little to learn about uneven development in the world
economy, although they have been more used to finding the
advantages rather than the disadvantages stacked in their
favour. Since they were the first nation to develop modern
industry and to embrace most whole-heartedly the new
division of labour it made possible, with all its consequences
for social structure, the British established a marked lead over
other states, even those like France which had initially a larger

population, a more extensive land area, and greater resources. Marx argued in a famous passage that 'the country that is more developed industrially only shows to the less developed the image of its own future'. He had England in mind, and it was the British model of development that countries like Germany strove to emulate and to surpass. The history of capitalism as a world economic and political system has involved not simply relentless competition between capitalist enterprises in their drive for high and secure profits. It has also increasingly involved competition between states. Nations have organised themselves to catch up with those states that have forged ahead, and nationalism has become an ideology for galvanising and reorganising societies to take advantage of the opportunities for military power and material wealth that industrialisation and the world economy have created. Once one country had industrialised and opened up a significant lead, all others were gradually drawn in to the race, for it became clear that catching up and keeping abreast was the price of any kind of national independence; states that could not, or would not, fell prey to imperialist penetration by the leading capitalist powers. Non-development came to mean underdevelopment and the incorporation of all such territories into the orbit of the dominant capitalist economies in ways that benefited those economies. The organisation of strong national state power in a given territory came to seem a necessary condition for ensuring an escape from underdevelopment and backwardness.[14]

The steady slide of the British economy, from a position of commanding superiority to a condition where some observers began to speculate whether Britain could be the first developed capitalist economy to become underdeveloped, prompts obvious questions. Why have the British been unable to organise a recovery? Why has there been no political reorganisation capable of enabling Britain, once it had fallen behind, to catch up? Why has the decline been so remorseless? Where is British nationalism? The decline has now been proceeding for a hundred years, half the period that industrial capitalism has existed in Britain. The panic that swept the British press and British ruling circles at the turn of the century about the rise of German and American industry, produced a stream of arguments and complaints very similar to those of the 1960s and 1970s.[15] British industry was technologically backward, uninterested in science, and staffed by mediocre managers; the scale of production was too small, and the amount of technical education inadequate. The British had become lazy, eager to consume, reluctant to work, and resistant to innovation. Fuelled by such books as E. M. Williams, *Made in Germany* (1896), A. Williamson, *British Industries and Foreign Competition* (1894) and F. A. Mackenzie, *American Invaders* (1902), as well as a vigorous campaign in the imperialist and protectionist press, widespread alarm about the penetration of foreign competition and its threat to British economic and ultimately political supremacy began to be voiced. A headline in the *Daily Mail* in 1900 summed up a characteristic theme: 'American Furniture in England. A further indictment of the trade unions'. Explanations for the growing British failure to match foreign competition began to dwell less on the supposed shoddiness of American and German goods and the subsidies that were held to make them cheap, and more on the short-comings in British social organisation. As the *Daily Mail* put it in 1901:

> At the risk of being thought unpatriotic this journal has persistently . . . called attention to the numberless blows administered to our commercial supremacy, chiefly by reason of the superior education methods and strenuous life of the American and the German.[16]

Such diagnoses of why Britain has fallen behind have prompted all manner of remedies. But the problem goes deeper than incorrect or insufficient policies. Whenever any particular feature of the British economy or British state is isolated and proclaimed to be the factor holding back the economy from performing more successfully, contrary evidence has never been long in coming to throw doubt on its importance.

Awareness of the nation's relative economic decline has come to dominate contemporary British politics. According to Martin Wiener 'the leading problem of modern British history is the explanation of economic decline'.[17] There is a growing realisation of the scale of the problem and the depth of the political failure to do anything about it. In his powerful polemic against the priorities of post-war economic policy Sidney Pollard writes:

> There is in operation . . . a law of the deterioration of British economic policies. Like the 'average' Russian harvest (worse than last year's, better than next year's) every government seems to have done more damage and to have succeeded in fewer things than the preceding one.[18]

The extent of the slide has been remarkable. From being the leading economy in western Europe in 1950 Britain had declined by 1980 to be one of the poorest. British output and productivity were little better than half the levels in comparable economies. The size of the gap that has opened in such a short time is astonishing. Pollard estimated in 1982 that if present trends continued, Britain would be overtaken by Greece, Portugal and Spain, and that the British economy would not reach the *present* level of national income enjoyed by the Federal Republic of Germany until 2051. The depreciation of sterling (against the dollar it has fallen from $4.03 after the war and stood at $1.56 in September 1989) reflects the relative impoverishment of the British economy.[19]

What is even more astonishing, however, is that a problem which received such sustained attention since the end of the 1950s and which produced so many new policies to remedy it should have proved so resistant to all the cures that were attempted. The problems appeared more intractable at the beginning of the 1980s than they were in the 1960s. Between 1979 and 1981 the economy was no longer merely in relative decline but actually began contracting. On some estimates unemployment reached 20 per cent of the labour force,[20] manufacturing output shrank to the levels of the mid-1960s and the public finances were under severe strain.

But has Britain actually declined? Is the decline real? Here there is an immediate paradox. The decline in Britain's world status and world power has been accompanied not by falling but by rising material wealth. The mass of British people were considerably better off in 1973 when Britain finally entered the EEC, as one of its poorer members, than they had been in 1900 when British power and economic superiority, though challenged, were still pre-eminent. Moreover, the performance of the British economy has steadily improved as the century has gone on. The annual rate of growth increased from 1 per cent between 1900 and 1913 to 2.3 per cent between 1922 and 1938 to 3.2 per cent between 1957 and 1965. The annual productivity increase in the same three periods was 0 per cent, 1.1 per cent and 2.4 per cent.[21] The period of loudest clamour about British decline actually turns out to be the period when the British economy has grown faster than at any time since 1870.

Is this decline? What has to be remembered are the different senses which are entangled in the word. Britain's decline can be most clearly perceived in the absolute decline of British dominance of the world economy – military, financial, and industrial. Britain's leading role was heavily qualified after the First World War. After the Second World War Britain, although still a world power, was no longer a major one, and its position dwindled still further as it shed its Empire and attempted to negotiate entry into the EEC. Decline as a process in British politics refers first to this loss of world power, the painful transition to a greatly reduced role and a greatly diminished capacity, and the corresponding alteration in national perspectives which had to result. This was an absolute decline because it involved an irreversible demotion to Britain from super-power status.

The second process involved in Britain's decline is not an absolute decline at all, but the relative economic decline that is apparent when British national economic performance is compared with that of its major industrial rivals, particularly the other states in the EEC, and Japan. Such a relative decline has been quite compatible with an absolute rise in production and productivity, whilst the world economy was growing and not stagnating. The idea of a relative decline is one of those notions which, like the rotation of the earth round the sun, appears to contradict common sense. As one of Shaw's practical men says of Copernicus: 'Can't the fellow use his eyes?'[22] The common experience has been not of declining but of rising living standards.

Certainly all measurements of decline must be treated with caution. There are great difficulties in measuring a national economy as though it were a single self-contained unit in the world economy. It is actually made up of a multitude of activities and relationships, many of them reaching beyond the arbitrary frontiers of the national territory. Within a national economy there is certain to be uneven development and an imbalance between different regions, different sectors, and different firms. Many individual companies and even whole regions can be prospering even whilst the economy as a whole is stagnating. Comparisons between national economies are notoriously difficult, since many indicators of performance, starting with GNP itself, can only be compared by assuming that the prevailing exchange rate between the two currencies is a reliable guide for measuring the size of one country's output in terms of the other. Similarly national income figures always leave out many things that are not traded on the market, so have no price, but can be decisive for living standards. One country might appear materially poorer but still be reckoned to enjoy a higher standard of living.[23]

But so long as the world economy contains within it separate territorial jurisdictions, comparisons between national economies will continue to be made. Despite all the qualifications, the relative decline of the British economy during the long boom, and the reason for its perilous condition after 1973 do stand out. The striking fact is not that there was no growth in the British economy, but that its rate of growth was less than that of the most technologically advanced economy, the United States. Whereas Germany, Japan and France all significantly closed the technological gap between themselves and the United States, Britain failed to do so. If anything the gap grew greater.[24]

The annual rate of growth of the British economy both in terms of output and output per head were significantly below all other major capitalist countries in the second decade of the long boom (see Table 1.1). Such a performance naturally had its effect upon the international growth league. In terms of Gross Domestic Product per head Britain slipped from ninth in 1961 to thirteenth in 1966 and fifteenth in 1971. By 1976 Britain was eighteenth, having fallen behind not just the

United States, Canada and Sweden, but Iceland, France, Finland, Austria, and Japan as well.[25]

Table 1.1   Rates of growth of GDP (Gross Domestic Product) 1962–72 (annual percentage rates)

	GDP	GDP *per capita*
France	4.7	5.7
West Germany	3.6	4.5
Italy	3.9	4.6
Japan	9.2	10.4
United States	3.0	4.2
United Kingdom	2.2	2.7

Source: OECD National Accounts 1961–72.

The most serious aspect of this relative decline which has often been highlighted is the erosion of the United Kingdom's position in wound manufacturing. The British share in world manufacturing output fell from 9.6 per cent in 1960 to 5.8 per cent in 1975.[26] Britain consistently failed to match the levels of productivity growth achieved in other countries (see Table 1.2). Gross Domestic Product per head in Germany in 1900 was 36 per cent below that in Britain. In 1973 it was 29 per cent higher. In Italy it was 63 per cent below Britain in 1900; by 1973 it was the same.[27] Many studies have confirmed this. The Central Policy Review Staff found that labour productivity on comparable vehicle models was 30 per cent below that in West Germany, France, and Italy.[28] Another study comparing labour productivity differences within international companies found that productivity levels in the United States and Canada were 50 per cent above those in Britain; West Germany was 27 per cent above, Italy 16 per cent above, and France 15 per cent above.[29] A major factor contributing to this has been the persistently low levels of investment in Britain, generally about half the levels of investment in manufacturing of Britain's major competitors. One study in 1978 estimated that the fixed assets per worker in manufacturing in the United Kingdom were only £7500, compared with £23 000 in West Germany and £30 000 in Japan.[30] Whereas in 1870 Britain enjoyed the highest

Table 1.2   Phases of productivity growth (GDP per man-hour), 1870–1976
(annual average compound growth rates)

	1870–1913	1913–50	1950–76
France	1.8	1.7	4.9
Germany	1.9	1.2	5.8
Italy	1.2	1.8	5.3
Japan	1.8	1.4	7.5
United States	2.1	2.5	2.3
United Kingdom	1.1	1.5	2.8

Source: A. Maddison, 'The Long Run Dynamics of Productivity Growth', in
W. Beckerman (ed.), *Slow Growth in Britain* (Oxford University Press, 1979) p.
195.

Table 1.3   Shares in the value of world exports of manufactures, 1950–79
(percentages)

	1899	1929	1937	1950	1960	1970	1977	1979
United Kingdom	33.2	22.9	21.3	25.5	16.5	10.8	9.3	9.7
France	–	–	–	9.9	9.6	8.7	9.9	10.5
Germany	–	–	–	7.3	19.3	19.0	29.8	29.8
Japan	–	–	–	3.4	6.9	11.7	15.4	13.6
United States	–	–	–	27.3	21.6	18.5	15.9	15.9

Sources: London and Cambridge Economic Service, *The British Economy, Key
Statistics* (London, 1970) and NIESR *Quarterly Bulletin*, May 1980.

productivity level amongst the major capitalist economies, by
1970 Britain had one of the lowest.

The failure to maintain superiority in productivity and in
manufacturing has caused a steep fall in the importance of the
British economy in the world economy and in its share of
world trade (see Table 1.3). The significance of this table is
not that the British share has declined, which might only be of
arithmetical significance, but that the shares of Germany and
Japan not only expanded greatly but were then maintained at
a much higher level. The French share also remained
constant. In terms of total trade (not just manufactures), West
Germany became the second largest trading nation in the

world in 1971,[31] and the first European nation to overtake
Britain since trade statistics began to be collected.

The effects of all this on the British economy became
increasingly sharp in the 1970s. Unemployment climbed
steeply in Britain and inflation accelerated while industrial
output stagnated. British performance was noticeably worse
than most other major capitalist economies. Its level of
unemployment was, until 1980, about average, but its record
on prices and output was significantly below, as Tables 1.4,
1.5 and 1.6 show. Real take-home pay virtually stagnated
also; in 1980 it had barely risen above the level it had reached
by the beginning of 1974.[32]

1.4 The debates of the intellectuals

(i) The debate on policy

Decline re-emerged as a major problem for economic policy
and as a major issue in political debate in the 1960s. During
the past hundred years the perception of decline, both
absolute decline in world power and relative economic
decline, was politically important in the years before 1914 and
again in the 1920s. But the context in which the problem re-
emerged was very different. The displacement of Britain as

Table 1.4   Unemployment (% rate standardised according to international definitions)

	United States	Japan	France	West Germany	Italy	United Kingdom
1972	5.4	1.4	2.7	0.8	6.3	4.1
1973	4.7	1.3	2.6	0.9	6.3	3.0
1974	5.4	1.4	2.8	1.5	5.3	2.9
1975	8.3	1.9	4.1	3.6	5.8	3.9
1976	7.5	2.0	4.4	3.6	6.6	5.6
1977	6.9	2.0	4.9	3.6	7.1	6.3
1978	5.9	2.2	5.2	3.5	7.2	6.1
1979	5.7	2.1	5.9	3.1	7.7	5.8

Source: *National Institute Economic Review*, vol. 92, May 1980, table 18.

Table 1.5 Inflation (% annual changes in consumer prices for selected countries 1967–78)

	All OECD	United States	Japan	West Germany	France	United Kingdom
1967	3.1	2.8	4.0	1.4	2.7	2.5
1968	4.0	4.2	5.3	2.9	4.5	4.7
1969	4.8	5.4	5.2	1.9	6.4	5.4
1970	5.6	5.9	7.7	3.4	4.8	6.4
1971	5.3	4.3	6.1	5.3	5.5	9.4
1972	4.8	3.3	4.5	5.5	6.2	7.1
1973	7.9	6.2	11.7	6.9	7.3	9.2
1974	13.4	11.0	24.5	7.0	13.7	16.0
1975	11.4	9.1	11.8	6.0	11.8	24.2
1976	8.6	5.8	9.3	4.5	9.6	16.5
1977	8.7	6.5	8.1	3.9	9.4	15.9
1978	7.9	7.7	3.8	2.6	9.1	8.3

Source: OECD, *Economic Outlook*, July 1979.

Table 1.6 Industrial production (1975 = 100)

	OECD	EEC	United States	Japan	France	West Germany	Italy	United Kingdom
1969	88	89	94	80	85	90	87	97
1970	91	93	91	91	89	96	92	97
1971	93	95	93	94	93	97	92	97
1972	99	99	102	101	100	101	96	99
1973	109	107	110	116	107	108	105	100
1974	109	106	110	112	110	106	110	105
1975	100	100	100	100	100	100	100	100
1976	109	108	111	111	109	107	112	103
1977	113	110	117	116	110	110	112	108
1978	118	112	124	123	113	113	116	111
1979	124	117	129	133	117	119	123	115

Source: *National Institute Economic Review*, vol. 92, May 1980.

the leading world power had happened and Britain was no longer at the centre of the world economy resisting challenges to its industrial, financial and commercial leadership, but was now obliged to accommodate to the necessity of surviving

within the new world economic order established by the
United States.

Economic decline became an issue after the 1959 election
because despite the successful reconstruction of the British
economy after the war, despite the initial relative strength of
the British economy compared with all other countries except
the United States, Britain's economic growth was markedly
slower than almost any other in Western Europe in the 1950s.
This was so despite the overall buoyancy of the economy
helped by the great surge of growth throughout the world
economy. One of the many strange features of the most recent
phase of British decline was that policy-makers first became
concerned with the problem again after a decade when the
British economy had performed better than at any time since
before 1880. Living standards had risen, unemployment had
rarely been above 1 per cent, and inflation was only 2–3 per
cent per annum.[33]

The reasons for the concern about this performance (which
in the inter-war years would have been hailed a remarkable
success) was the much better performance that was achieved
elsewhere, the awareness of the extra wealth that was being
lost and the undermining of what remained of Britain's
political and economic importance in the world. The anxiety
about Britain's post-imperial future erupted in a flood of 'state
of England' writing which investigated every British institution and ranged in attitude from bleak pessimism to enthusi-
astic social engineering.

The debate on economic policy was much narrower than
this. There remained broad agreement on the framework and
objectives of economic policy. The commitment to an open
economy was the unquestioned assumption of foreign
economic policy, the acceptance of the balance between public
and private sectors and labour and capital shaped industrial
policy, while the commitment to balance total effective
demand with total resources defined the aims of stabilisation
policy: full employment, stable prices, a surplus on the
balance of payments, and economic growth.

The modernisation strategy of the 1960s did not question
these broad commitments or the balance of power between
labour and capital and the enlarged public sector on which

they were founded. The policy debate centred on whether the right balance of policies was being struck. In foreign economic policy the major doubts concerned the importance given to maintaining a surplus on the balance of payments in order to fund overseas military spending and foreign investments. It was argued by a long line of critics that the financial burden of maintaining key aspects of Britain's former world role were out of all proportion to their benefits because they imposed deflation on the domestic economy and hindered expansion.[34] British policy in the 1950s and 1960s gave major priority not to maintaining full employment which would have been high regardless of what governments did[35] but to achieving a quite unnecessary balance of payments target.

Most of the economists who made this criticism of British policy argued that it would be best for this burden to be removed altogether and for Britain to give up its 'delusions of grandeur'. But many also argued that even if this were not possible it would still be preferable to devalue the pound, or float it, or borrow to finance temporary deficits, rather than deflate the domestic economy by cutting back investment in order to protect the pound. The main explanation they gave for the relatively slow growth of the British economy was the greater priority which policy-makers gave to the balance of payments rather than to economic growth.

The strength of this case has never been seriously dented. The importance which policy-makers attached to the defence of sterling and to achieving a satisfactory balance of payments is not in dispute, and it is clear from the crude trade statistics that without the massive deficit on capital account and on government account the British economy would not have suffered balance of payments problems in any of the years that sparked sterling crises in the 1950s and 1960s.[36]

Yet although this diagnosis formed so central a part of the modernisation strategy of the 1964 Labour government it was never acted upon. For many economists the failure to devalue in 1964 was the main reason for the eventual failure of the entire modernisation strategy. Other economists have pointed out that devaluation when it did come in 1967 was no panacea, nor did the removal of the balance of payments constraint in 1972 (when the pound was floated) propel the

economy into rapid and sustained growth. But the critics of
the bipartisan foreign economic policy argue that for the
twenty years during which world output, productivity, and
investment of the western capitalist economy grew more
rapidly than ever before, British governments persistently
pursued a policy which held back investment and destroyed
industrial confidence. By 1970 British productivity had fallen
behind its main rivals and British industry was seriously
under-equipped.

There were other features of the modernisation strategy,
linked very often to the overall critique of post-war foreign
economic policy. In stabilisation policy many economists
argued that the fine-tuning of demand practised by the
authorities had increased rather than moderated fluctuations
in output. There was strong condemnation of the restrictive
policies which the stop–go cycle involved and there was
considerable support for a policy of sustained expansion. The
main debate centred on whether the risk of higher inflation
which such a policy introduced was better dealt with by
creating more 'slack' in the economy or by attempting to plan
prices and incomes. In both cases the aim remained the same
– to produce a steady and sustainable expansion of demand
which would remain in balance with the growth of productive
potential. Such analyses implied that the central problem for
the British economy was its tendency to 'overheat'. This was a
direct consequence of the full employment objective and led to
continued inflationary pressure which was one factor in the
crises of financial confidence in sterling, which were only kept
in check by periodic deflation. This suggested that any policy
which could control inflation might help to avoid the necessity
of imposing deflationary measures to maintain financial
confidence. So the demand-pull/cost-push debate on inflation
and the different prescriptions associated with it became an
important subsidiary explanation of why Britain had declined,
and why sustained expansion was so difficult to achieve. If
inflation could be mastered either by an incomes policy or by
a slight increase in unemployment, then the obstacles in the
path of faster expansion would be greatly reduced.

Many economists also argued, however, that what was
wrong with post-war Keynesian stabilisation policy was that

its chief purpose was to manipulate demand, withdrawing from any attempt to plan or directly influence supply. Many advocates of modernisation in the 1960s favoured an active supplyside industrial policy. This included measures to raise investment both in new plant in particular sectors and in particular regions; measures to encourage mergers and industrial rationalisation; measures to improve the rate at which new technologies were designed, developed and introduced; and measures involving many major new public spending programmes to increase investment in the infrastructure of the economy, especially in transport, health, and education.

The argument behind such proposals was that Britain was failing to achieve faster growth because it lacked the close links between government and industry which all other successful economies had established. The French model of indicative planning was greatly favoured in the early 1960s, and it was one of the main inspirations for the National Plan with its 4 per cent per annum growth target.

The high hopes that were attached to modernisation were disappointed. The constraint of the balance of payments was not evaded, inflation was not held down either by incomes policy or higher employment, and the supply-side bottlenecks were not eliminated.[37] Wages were held down, however, public expenditure was increased faster than planned (because 4 per cent economic growth was expected) and taxation rose, while profits were severely squeezed. The main result of the various modernisation programmes appeared to be the creation of profitless prosperity; a continuing stagnation of investment, output and productivity, and increase in industrial militancy and inflationary expectations. All these consequences came to a head in the years of the Health government – the last attempt, as it proved, to achieve an expansion of the economy within the post-war framework of economic management.[38]

The inquests on the years of the successive attempts at modernisation between 1960 and 1973 took place against a background of the end of the boom and the re-emergence of world recession and much slower growth after 1973. Britain's weaknesses, accumulated but also partly disguised in the years of boom, were dramatically exposed. The debate on

policy among economists became more complicated as wider
divergences of opinion emerged among them.

One approach focused on foreign economic policy, arguing
that it was the degree of openness of the national economy
maintained by all British governments which was chiefly to
blame for the failure to pursue a successful expansionist policy
at home. It advocated controls on capital movements and
either controls on trade or a very sizeable devaluation in order
to create the external conditions necessary for internal
reconstruction and growth.[39] Achieving internal growth in the
economy was not regarded as a very difficult matter so long as
the external constraint was removed. The openness of the
British economy was regarded as the main problem not
because the balance of payments or the pound still dominated
domestic policy, but because twenty years of stop–go succeeded
by world recession and international monetarism had left the
British economy hopelessly uncompetitive – its manufacturing
base threatened by rising levels of import penetration, its
export of capital increasing, its level of investment and
productivity well below international levels. The study has
already been cited which estimated that Britain would need to
spend £100 000 million to bring the level of capital equipment
per worker up to the level of its main competitors.[40] On this
kind of analysis the central problem was how to insulate the
British economy for long enough to enable it to regain
international competitiveness.

A very different approach came from those who emphasised
stabilisation policy. Here the major new theory was monetarism which rejected Keynesianism as a framework for policy,
particularly the idea that policy-makers should try to manipulate the total level of demand in the economy or try to strike a
balance between inflation and unemployment, or the balance
of payments and growth. Monetarism involved firstly a
specific doctrine about the causes of inflation – it argued that
there was a link between the growth of the stock of money and
the rate of increase in prices in the medium term – and
secondly a series of prescriptions about economic policy such
as the injunction that control of inflation should be government's main policy priority, and that neither unemployment
nor growth targets could be achieved by direct government

action or traded for a particular inflation rate. Only when sound money had been restored could full employment and sustainable economic growth be achieved again.[41]

Monetarist economists blamed Britain's decline chiefly on the failure of governments to control inflation and the pursuit of targets for employment and growth by manipulating demand which had led periodically to unsustainable booms and accelerating inflation. The failure to control public spending was a subsidiary theme. On this reasoning it was always the acceleration of inflation in the past that made sustainable growth impossible to achieve and led to the cumulative weakening of industrial capacity and the un-checked growth of the public sector.[42] If macro-economic policy had been different and inflation controlled, the economy could have grown at a faster rate.

Despite the growing influence of monetarism in the 1970s there were still many Keynesians who argued that it was not demand management that was the problem, but the failure to sustain a permanent incomes policy. There was a sharp division of opinion among economists as to whether mone-tarism would work and whether any success it might have in reducing inflation was the result not of control of the money supply but of higher unemployment and the destruction of industrial capacity.[43] There was a similar debate on the effectiveness of incomes policy and whether all such policies would eventually break down.[44]

Both Keynesians and monetarists often pursued their differences into the debates within the third perspective, which gave primary emphasis to industrial policy and argued that the real shortcoming in British economic policy had been the lack of an effective supply-side policy. But there was no agreement on what an effective supply-side policy might be (particularly since those developed in the 1960s apparently yielded so little). Opinion ranged all the way from those who emphasised market rigidities and called for the curbing of union power to make labour markets work freely again, and for taxes and welfare benefits to be reduced to restore incentives to enterprise and work, to those who advocated much greater state involvement in industry to identify and encourage present and future leading secors.[45]

(ii) The historical debates

British decline has passed through several phases. It has never been a single uniform process, because the definition of the problem and the remedies for it have changed. Each phase is marked out by a particular debate about the nature of the decline. The crucial context for each debate is the world order and Britain's place within it. It is this that ties together Britain's absolute decline as a Great Power with Britain's relative decline in economic power.

There are three key debates on decline that can be identified in British politics in the last hundred years. They are best characterised by their main themes – National Efficiency, Modernisation, and Social Democracy.

National Efficiency The first debate, on national efficiency, developed between 1880 and 1914 in response to the growing challenge from Germany and the United States to the exceptional position of military and economic strength which Britain had built up during the nineteenth century. Britain seemed ill-prepared for a major military contest with its challengers. The blame was put on the shortcomings of British economic performance and the inertia of Britain's traditional liberal, *laissez-faire* policy regime. The lack of organisation and planning of British resources was cited by Social Imperialists, New Liberals, and Fabian Socialists as the basic problem that had to be remedied.[46]

The pace of advance of German and American companies in some sectors was taken as evidence that Britain was lagging behind in the development of new products and new industries, that its costs were often higher, and that its techniques of marketing and selling goods and services were backward. Recent research has indicated that British pre-dominance was threatened directly only in a few spheres, but the spectre of Germany and the United States leapfrogging over Britain in industrial output and productivity fuelled a major political debate.

What worried the Social Imperialists were the consequences of the changing balance of economic power in the world economy for the political and military balance.

Britain was recognised to be particularly vulnerable because of its small land base and therefore limited physical and human resources of the British Isles itself compared to the much larger potential of the continental sized economies.

Britain ruled over a greater population and a greater land area than any other power in 1900, but the British Empire was a highly diverse and fragmented political entity. It compared unfavourably with the concentration of resources and territory enjoyed by both Germany and the United States. It was impossible for Britain to extend its immediate heartland, and indeed even part of that – Ireland was seriously disaffected.

The Social Imperialists advocated public programmes to remedy deficiencies in education, health, housing, and social security. They sought to weld the British Empire into a much more cohesive political and economic bloc. British industry would be partially safeguarded from competition by the imposition of a tariff, the proceeds of which would pay for the new spending programmes. The physical and human resources of the Empire would be much more consciously organised to promote increasing integration and common purpose. Britain's problem was that in the new era of organised capitalism only powers with access to vast physical and human resources could maintain their standing as Great Powers. If Britain could not mobilise such resources through its Empire, it seemed doomed to lose its preeminence.[47]

Modernisation The debate on modernisation emerged in the altered context of world politics that was created by the First World War and the entry of the United States on the side of Britain and France. England and Germany were severely weakened by the war while American power and influence were enormously enhanced. After 1917 it soom became clear that Britain's traditional naval predominance would never be restored, that her financial strength had been significantly undermined, and that it was no longer possible for Britain by herself to establish and maintain the conditions for a liberal world economic order. The attempt to restore the gold standard and with it pre-war prosperity proved illusory and collapsed in 1931.

What opened therefore in 1917 was a long period of often uneasy relationship between Britain and the United States during which British political opinion eventually became reconciled to the United States assuming the roles which Britain had once performed in establishing and sustaining a liberal world order. Britain came to occupy a subordinate although still important place within this new order which fully emerged in the 1940s.

The negotiated transfer of hegemony which took place between these two Great Powers was unprecedented and by no means smooth. Britain at many points resisted American demands and fought for its own interests, and the preservation of its Empire. The debate on Britain's relationship with the United States continued into the 1960s and the withdrawal from the last of Britain's colonies, but it was already clear by 1950 that a bipartisan consensus had emerged on the importance of the alliance with the United States as the cornerstone of British policy.[48]

Throughout this period a key theme of the domestic political debate was how Britain could modernise itself, to stay abreast of the economy that was increasingly perceived as the world leader, the United States. The need to modernise was accepted both by those who hoped to maintain British world status by retaining the Empire, and by those who came to see Britain's future lying firmly within the American orbit.

The main thrust of the debate, building in part on the earlier arguments about national efficiency, was collectivist. The objective was to modernise British industrial structure, by changing the relationship between state and industry and the character and extent of state intervention. The deep-seated social conflicts and tensions of the period between 1880 and 1920 had given way to a period of greater stability. The shape of a domestic compromise between capital and labour which laid the basis for the reforms of the 1940s had begun to emerge.[49]

The advocates of modernisation in all parties increasingly urged the adoption in Britain of the institutions and practices of Fordism, the political and industrial system pioneered in the United States, which was based on mass production and large production units and required the state to play an increased role in regulating and sustaining it.[50]

The extension of public responsibility, the growth of corporatist institutions for handling industrial relations, the acceptance of a Keynesian framework for managing the economy – none of these were accepted without considerable effort and political struggle. But the adoption of American methods of industrial relations and work organisation in many key industries proceeded quite rapidly during the 1930s. These were then consolidated by the political and legal changes of the 1940s. A full Fordist regime appeared to have emerged in Britain under the banners of collectivism, planning, and welfare.

Despite the apparent success of the British economy during the 1950s, however, evidence began to accumulate by the end of the decade that the British economy was growing much more slowly than other industrial economies. The debate on modernisation was renewed in the 1960s. The modernisation and reconstruction of the 1930s and 1940s had apparently failed to produce an economy that was internationally competitive in the new post-war international order.

This perception that Britain was still performing less well than comparable economies became a dominant issue in the 1960s and produced a great deal of diagnosis and many new policies and spending programmes aimed at remedying the deficiencies and closing the gap. But the issue was debated within the framework and assumptions that the leaderships of both main parties had accepted since at least 1945 and in some respects since the 1920s.[51]

Social Democracy The third debate, from the late 1960s up to the present, has focused on social democracy, its failures and limitations, its responsibility for decline. It too arose in a new altered context of world order, whose most important features were the challenges to American leadership of the world system, the end of the long boom in the world economy, the increasing pace of internationalisation, and the entry of Britain into the European Community.

The domestic compromise between labour and capital which had sustained the British polity for more than forty years broke down and its disappearance called into question the social democratic order that had been grafted on to Britain's old constitutional state.

The catalyst for the new debate on decline was the failure of successive governments to deliver the fruits of modernisation they had promised. The evident inability to arrest the relative economic decline did not at first harm living standards, which continued to rise, but had an increasingly severe impact on inflation and unemployment. Government authority was weakened, both main parties for a time lost support, and in the 1970s some thought democracy itself was at risk.

The debate on social democracy produced a polarisation of political argument, which included the revival of a socialist critique of British capitalism and its failings, the restatement of anti-collectivist arguments on the Right, and the emergence of a strong Centre critique of the impact of class-based politics on British economic performance.[52]

(iii) Four theses on decline

Underlying these debates on decline are four main theses: the imperial thesis, the cultural thesis, the supply-side thesis, and the democratic thesis. Each focuses on a different aspect of social structure – the world system, the cultural order, the economy, and the political system – in developing their explanation of decline. Each thesis has a number of variants corresponding to the three leading perspectives in political economy: market, state and class. The different explanations are summarised in Table 1.7.

These three perspectives provide not just explanations of decline but also assist the elaboration of programmes for reversing it. In this way they become a vital component of political strategies. Each perspective offers at least one version of each of the four central theses on decline.

Each thesis seeks to explain why the British economy has performed relatively poorly during the twentieth century. The imperial thesis lays the blame on Britain's world role, which led to an overextension of British power and the undermining of domestic economic performance. It sees decline as a result of the slowness with which Britain adjusted to its changed

Table 1.7 Theories of decline

	MARKET	STATE	CLASS
WORLD SYSTEM the imperial thesis: Britain's world role undermined the domestic economy	legacies of empire i. lack of exposure to international competition ii. protectionism, subsidy iii. abandonment of gold standard	overextension of British state i. military ii. financial iii. foreign investment iv. misguided foreign economic policy	character of British capitalism i. divided capitalism city/industry split ii. global capitalism
ECONOMY the supply-side thesis: state/economy relations weakened the manufacturing sector	economic management i. wrong macro-economic policy – Keynesianism ii. public spending public sector too large; taxes too high iii. too interventionist industrial strategy iv. trade union power	developmental state i. inadequacy of Keynesianism ii. lack of coordination between government, industry, and finance iii. poor industrial relations iv. no consistent industrial strategy v. bias and size of spending on infrastructure	state/economy relations i. incomplete Fordism; unsuccessful corporatism; inadequate investment coordination; poor industrial relations ii. class stalemate
POLITY the state thesis: Britain's state was too weak to promote modernisation	weak state i. deficiencies of political market ii. excessive expectations iii. distributional coalitions; institutional sclerosis iv. political business cycle	weak state i. overload ii. adversary politics – lack of effectiveness – inadequate representation	weak state i. ancien regime ii. dual crisis of the state iii. exhaustion of social democracy
CULTURE the cultural thesis: Britain's political culture held back modernisation	anti-enterprise anti-capitalist culture i. welfare dependency ii. elite culture and attitudes iii. egalitarianism	anti-industrial culture i. institutions of British Establishment ii. liberal ethos	anti-modernisation culture i. aristocratic ethos ii. Labourism

status in the world and shed the burdens and attitudes and policies which the world role had left behind.

The supply-side thesis concentrates on the relative backwardness of British manufacturing, which it ascribes either to an inadequate relationship between the state and the economy or to a balance of power between the classes that has produced stalemate. Britain acquired Fordism but it was flawed and incomplete.

The state thesis shifts the focus to the institutions of the British state and why the organisation of this state makes it very difficult for British governments to carry through programmes of long-term modernisation. The state appears weak because it has proved neither effective nor representative.

Finally the cultural thesis sees the main cause of British decline in the existence of a deep-rooted anti-industrial political culture, which has created powerful resistance to modernisation and change, and perpetuated many traditionalist aspects of British society.

The Market Perspective (1) *imperial thesis*: The market version of the imperial thesis emphasises the distortions which empire and a world political role introduced into the workings of the British economy. The specific costs are seen as the retreat from free trade into imperial protection in the 1930s, the abandonment of the gold standard, and the growth of subsidy and other forms of internal protectionism, which gradually sealed off the domestic economy from international competition. A further burden was provided by the level of overseas government spending, much of it military spending, which helped to unbalance the British balance of payments, and contributed to the sterling crises and stop–go cycles of the 1950s and 1960s.[53]

(2) *supply-side thesis*: From the market perspective the failure of British governments to develop a successful supply-side policy is closely linked to the adoption of a mistaken macro-economic policy – Keynesian demand management – which raised the goals of full employment and economic growth to the same status as stable prices.

The market version of the supply-side thesis therefore starts from the monetarist and Austrian critiques of Keynesianism. The restoration of sound money is vital so that attention can be directed to the supply-side factors which affect output and productivity. Restoring sound money requires not just the replacement of Keynesian by monetarist macro-economic policies, but also a substantial reduction in public expenditure. The public sector is regarded as much too large, both in terms of spending programmes and of the size of the public enterprise sector. The number and level of programmes need reducing, to curtail government involvement in the economy and to make possible a substantial reduction in taxation.[54]

Keynesianism is linked in the market perspective with high public spending and interventionist industrial policies, which prevent markets from clearing and reduce competition by imposing controls and providing subsidies. The result is to produce a fettered market economy which performs poorly because the price mechanism is prevented from guiding economic activity. The relationship between state and economy is responsible for decline because the state is too interventionist and does not confine itself to guaranteeing and policing the market order.[55]

The market is fettered in a further way. Another version of the supply-side thesis identifies the problem at the heart of British decline in the relationship between capital and labour. From the market perspective the problem is that the trade unions are too powerful, and use their power to distort prices and to uphold restrictive practices which reduce the efficiency of production and create overmanning.[56]

(3) *state thesis*: The extension of the state beyond its proper limits has made it weak and ineffective. The stability and longevity of Britain's political institutions have produced institutional sclerosis as special interests have multiplied.[57] The way the political market works has led to continuous interference in the economic market. Some market theorists have suggested that a political business cycle has developed, through which politicians attempt to ensure re-election by manipulating the economy to create prosperity just before elections. Others have emphasised the damage to the market order caused by the generation of excessive expectations about

what governments can deliver, as a result of the competitive overbidding by the political parties.[58]

The political market is regarded as much more imperfect than economic markets. Voters lack a budget constraint and this makes them irresponsible in the way they cast their votes, since they can opt for the programme which offers them the greatest benefits without having to bear all or sometimes any of the costs. This process leads to a persistent bias towards the growth of government and interference in the workings of free markets. The state is too weak to assert a public interest, which from the market perspective is the enforcing of a market order in which general rules govern all individual exchanges, and arbitrary interventions by public bodies are minimised.

(4) *cultural thesis*: Cultural hostility to capitalism and enterprise are regarded as important factors in the decline. The source of this hostility is traced to the dominance of anti-market and collectivist ideas in key sections of the intellectual and political élite. A political culture developed which put a ·lower priority on production, incentives and enterprise, than on egalitarian redistribution, collective welfare and social solidarity. It was diffused through key institutions such as the civil service, the universities, the schools, the media, and the Labour movement. The low cultural value placed on risk-taking and profit-making acted as a persistent obstacle to creating a more dynamic economy, and perpetuated instead the development of a culture in which large numbers of individuals were encouraged to become dependent on collective provision.[59]

The State Perspective The state perspective views the process of historical change through the structures and institutions of the state.

(1)*imperial thesis*: British decline is here attributed to the overextension of British power. One version argues that there is a trade-off between economic growth, domestic consumption, and military security. States rise to be great powers by maintaining a balance between all three, but once they have achieved a position of dominance and leadership, they steadily lose the ability to maintain that balance. Most often they give greater priority to military security and domestic consumption than to economic growth, and fall victim to rising states which can afford to be more single-minded in their pursuit of economic success.[60]

There have been many explanations of Britain's relative economic decline as a consequence of the effort devoted to maintaining Britain's global role, both as a military and imperial power, and as the world's leading financial power. A higher priority was placed on keeping sterling strong and maintaining overseas military spending and foreign investment than on domestic economic reconstruction and modernisation.[61]

(2) *supply-side thesis*: A development state has failed to emerge in Britain. The contrast here is with the success of many other economies in moving beyond either a regulatory form of state or a central planning regime to an active interventionist state which promotes continual modernisation and economic growth. What has been stressed in numerous studies is the poor co-ordination between government, industry and finance in Britain compared with many other countries. British governments as a result have failed to develop either a consistent or an effective industrial strategy.[62]

They have also failed to remedy persistent British short-comings in strategic spending on infrastructure, research and development, and training to promote modernisation and economic development. In industrial relations the lack of a developmental state has meant a persistent failure to incorporate the trade-union movement fully into national and industrial decision-making with damaging consequences in terms of macro-economic management, strikes and restrictive practices.

(3) *state thesis*: The lack of a developmental state is reflected in the character of the state in Britain, which makes it both ineffective and unrepresentative. It is ineffective because it has become overloaded through the multiplication of tasks and functions beyond its capacity to discharge them. It is unrepresentative both because the incorporation of major interests into national decision-making has never been complete, and because the simple plurality electoral system has encouraged the development of an adversary style of two-

party politics, which has created discontinuity in economic policy and frustrated the achievement of consensus.[63]

(4) *cultural thesis*: The anti-industrial political culture arises from the nature of the British Establishment, and the ethos of its institutions, particularly the public schools, the old universities, the civil service, the Monarchy, and the aristocracy. There is an orientation towards commerce and finance but not towards industry. This is reflected in the low status accorded industry and engineering in comparison with the professions.

In sharp contrast to the market perspective the low value placed on economic growth and modernisation reflects the persistence of a liberal ethos which accords a limited role for the state in the management of industrial modernisation.[64] The ambivalence of the British political élite to economic growth meant that the preservation of the values, status, and lifestyle of the British Establishment tended to be given higher priority.[65]

The Class Perspective The class perspective makes class organisation of the economy and society the key factor in explaining historical and political development.

(1) *imperial thesis*: Class versions of the imperial thesis have emphasised how the character of British economic development imbued British capital with a strong international orientation. There has been dispute over whether this reflects the interests of all the leading sections of British capital or whether it reflects the long-term hegemony exercised by the financial sector in Britain over manufacturing industry.[66]

The degree of institutional autonomy enjoyed by the financial sector in Britain has always been exceptional and predates Britain's industrial predominance in the nineteenth century. It reflects a much older feature of the relationship of the British economy to the world economy, the British role as a financial and commercial intermediary in world trade. The priority given to this role by British governments made British imperialism predominantly a free-trade imperialism, and entailed the subordination of domestic interests or their incorporation into British external expansion.

(2) *supply-side thesis*: Britain's weak manufacturing sector is an aspect of Britain's failure to develop a successful Fordist regime of accumulation. Those countries that did, created a variety of institutional means, including a developmental state, to establish close relations between the state, industrial companies, the banks, and the trade unions. Britain had some aspects necessary for a successful Fordism, such as Keynesian demand management, but its supply-side policies were very inadequate, and showed in poor industrial performance and poor industrial relations.[67]

A different class version of the supply-side thesis focuses not on the regime of accumulation but on the balance of power between classes. The cause of decline is class stalemate. The working class in Britain has achieved sufficient defensive strength to frustrate the desire of management to modernise plants and reduce manning levels. This argument echoes the analysis from a market perspective of the effects of trade-union power, but the two perspectives diverge not only over the remedy for this situation but over who was to blame for it.[68]

(3) *state thesis*: The inability of the British state to carry through modernisation is traced to its historical origins, and to the absence from British history since the twentieth century of the thoroughgoing reconstruction of the state which all other major capitalist countries experienced either as a result of revolution or invasion. The British *ancien régime* perpetuated a set of institutions and a set of élites which left British governments without the organisational means to carry through modernisation. Instead there was a consensus throughout the British state against modernisation.[69]

Other class analyses of the British state have put less emphasis on its pre-modern character, but have focused rather on its development in the last hundred years. Between 1880 and 1930 the liberal state was engulfed by a series of major crises. The solutions and compromises that were worked out to these crises moved the state some way towards social democracy, but never led to a major reconstruction. Social democracy as a result remained incomplete; corporatism was not successfully established nor was a developmental state.[70] This led in due course to a dual crisis, a crisis of the representative institutions of the state – the parties and parliament – which no longer ensured representation; and a crisis of the corporatist institutions of the state, because the national economic policy was not achieving results.[71]

(4) *cultural thesis*: The character of British capitalism and the British state are reflected in the political culture. The aristocratic ethos of the British Establishment and the Labourist ethos of the working class combine to reinforce the consensus against modernisation. The weakness of manufacturing in relation to finance is reflected in the cultural subordination of the former, and its failure to articulate its own programme and values. Culture is not a prime mover in the class perspective, but it acts as a very effective cement of an order which is incapable of reforming itself.[72]

1.5 Conclusion

The intellectual debates on Britain's decline have produced no agreement on either causes or remedies. The problems are intractable and resistant to conventional policy-making. But the debates have succeeded in highlighting the special historical features which mark British capitalism out from more successful national capitalisms elsewhere. There is firstly the international role of the British state and the way in which the national economy is integrated into the world economy; secondly the nature of the British state and its institutional relationships with the economy and society; thirdly the formation of the British working class and the manner and extent of its incorporation into British society. These three problems form the subject matter of Chapters 2 and 3.

Numerous studies have shown how decline cannot be reduced to technical issues and remedies. There is considerable agreement that Britain's problems lie in what are known as 'supply-side factors'. The Brookings report on the British economy at the end of the 1970s, a follow-up to their earlier report some twelve years before, rejected all conventional technical explanations which point to shortcomings in policy,

and concluded sorrowfully that 'Britain's economic malaise
stems largely from its productivity problem whose origins lie
deep in the social system'.[73] It is deep into that social system
and particularly into its external relations that we must now
go.

PART II

HISTORY

2
The world island

We can with safety make one prophecy: whatever the
outcome of this war, the British Empire is at an end. It
has been mortally wounded. The future of the British
people is to die of hunger and tuberculosis on their
cursed island.

Adolf Hitler[1]

Britain's decline can only be understood, indeed only
exists, in relation to the world economic system of which
Britain is a part. This chapter considers the history of the
expansion of the British state, and the consequences for
Britain's subsequent progress of the relatively slender base
of population and resources upon which its massive world
empire was established. All understanding begins here, for
this is the feature that most clearly marks Britain off from
other states.

2.1 The expansion of England

The expansion of England was a twofold process. There was
first the expansion within the territorial limits of the British
Isles, which created a unified English state. This state
eventually succeeded in extending its control over all parts
of the British Isles by military conquest of Wales and
Ireland and unification with Scotland. The English state
became Great Britain in 1707 and the United Kingdom in
1801.[2] But even while this process was being completed it

was overshadowed by the external expansion of this state, the creation of a Greater Britain beyond the British Isles in the New World. The ability to seize opportunities that the emerging world economy was creating was greatly improved by the organisation of a strong national state secure in its own territory.

What is so striking about the process of English expansion within the British isles is how a state was eventually formed which, though composed of several nations, came to enjoy exceptional internal unity and cohesion. The major divisions which have so undermined the legitimacy of other states, divisions between regions, between religious groups, between races and between nationalities, have not been absent in Britain but have certainly been less important. One major reason for this lies in the successful organisation of a strong and centralised public power by the Yorkist Kings, and subsequently by the Tudors in the sixteenth century, which helped to moderate and contain internal conflicts. The subordination of nobility and then church to the royal authority, following the Wars of the Roses and the English Reformation, removed two major obstacles to the authority of the state and to its ability to frame laws and enforce them throughout its territory. It also increased its capacity to defend and extend that territory. In the sixteenth century the English state strove to consolidate its hold on Wales and Ireland, principally because the territorial integrity of England was seen to require English control of all parts of the British Isles, to deny possible bases for internal or external challenges.

The same considerations governed the attitude of the English towards the Scots. Even after the Union of the Crowns in 1603 Scotland remained a separate state, potentially threatening to England, not only because of the possibility that the Scots might act independently and in conflict with English interests, but also because in any such conflict Scotland might well ally with a foreign power against England. This possibility was ended by the Act of Union in 1707, which united the two Parliaments. It allowed the Scots to retain many of their own institutions, including their legal system, their church and their schools, and restored complete free trade and access by the Scots to the developing English commercial Empire. Henceforward the expansion of the new state was to be directed from a single centre, and the Parliament at Westminster became the central symbol and institution for maintaining its legitimacy.

One factor which greatly aided the successful unification of Wales and Scotland with England was the dominance of the English nation, the absence of clear racial or ethnic differences, and the overwhelming dominance of Protestantism. In terms of population and resources the English far outweighed the other nations, and English institutions, English agriculture and English industry were generally more developed. The rapid expansion of the English state abroad after 1650, and the industrialisation of its economy at home, certainly aided the integration of the three nations into a cohesive multinational state, whose centre was in London. All three nations developed along similar lines in the nineteenth century. By 1900 all had major centres of industry, all had a similar distribution of their working population between industry and agriculture, and a similar balance between the cities and the country. All were integrated into the same unified national market and the extended world market. All had in consequence a similar level of income per head and a similar rate of economic growth.[3]

The great exception to this harmonious pattern of development was Ireland, which was never assimilated, never integrated, and which prevented the kingdom ever being truly united. The history of relations between Ireland and the rest of Britain highlights how accidental and fortunate the smooth integration of the rest of the United Kingdom actually was.[4] Ireland was treated as a colony from the beginning, its military conquest being completed under the Tudors. Determined efforts were made to establish settlers on the same lines as the settlements in the New World. The settlers were alien in culture and in religion, which helped intensify the division between Ireland and Britain. The seventeenth-century civil war and the settlement of 1688, while laying the foundations for the rise of Great Britain, also prepared the way for the eventual separation of Ireland. The backing given by the Catholic Irish for Charles I and James II led to the reconquest of the country first by Cromwell and then by William III. Huge confiscations of land were made and an Anglo-Irish Protestant land-owning class established to rule over the Catholic peasantry. Ireland was denied free trade with the rest of Britain and all competition from Irish industry and Irish agriculture was prevented. As a result Ireland never achieved the same kind of industrial and social development as the rest of the United Kingdom, except in the area around Belfast where Protestant settlers were particularly concentrated. The bulk of Ireland remained poor and backward, frequently devastated by famines and milked by the huge annual tribute in rents which flowed across the Irish Sea, while suffering enormous emigration both to Britain and the United States.[5] It is hardly surprising that Ireland was the country that saw the first sustained nationalist revolt against British imperial rule since the rebellion of the American colonists.

What was so significant about the Irish problem in the nineteenth century was the complete inability of the governing class in Britain to handle it. So explosive did the Home Rule issue become in British politics that it produced some major political realignments,[6] and so deep a split within the governing class that it almost ended in open defiance of the authority of the Westminster government by sections of the army and the Unionist party. Only the First World War averted what could have been a major rupture in British constitutional development.[7] The history of the Irish problem shows how great an advantage constitutional legitimacy gave the British state, because it placed the British state upon a foundation so much more secure than many others, and made internal politics so much more manageable. It was not a matter of the innate skill of the governing class that Britain had so tranquil a development. That was due far more to certain structural features of the British position which made possible the integration of Wales, Scotland and England and which were lacking in the case of Ireland. Most important of all was the opportunity

of sharing and participating in the overseas expansion of
the British state.

2.2 The drive to empire

The building of a state that was secure in its territory,
internally unified, and whose constitution enjoyed legitimacy over the greater part of its territory, was assisted by
the successful expansion overseas, and in turn aided it. This
expansion, which began to accelerate after 1650, was by no
means inevitable, and little in previous British history
anticipated it. England had been an unimportant and
distant colony of the Roman Empire and subsequently a
minor medieval kingdom, always on the fringes of European
politics, culture and trade, never at the centre. The
transformation of this island kingdom, in the course of two
centuries, into an imperial power of unprecedented dimensions, shaped British politics irrevocably and brought a
fundamental shift in British perspectives and British preoc-
cupations.

In the Middle Ages Britain was a continental power, its
kings pursued dynastic ambitions in Europe, and the
country was wholly contained within European culture and
European horizons. It was the discovery of the New World
which transformed its position. The overseas expansion of
Europe was begun by the Portuguese and the Spaniards in
the fifteenth century, and created a new transatlantic world
economy based around protected colonies and protected
trade. Once established it provided opportunities for many
other states, particularly Holland, France and Britain, and
encouraged a competitive struggle for territory and wealth
from which Britain ultimately secured by far the greatest
returns.[8]

One principal reason why the British were able to benefit
was that the creation of a world economy which spanned
oceans, rather than merely an inland sea like the Mediterra-
nean, greatly favoured those states able to develop sea
power. Two-thirds of the earth's surface is covered by sea,
most of its states have coastlines, and every part of the

ocean is accessible from every other part. Few other states
had the security of an island base as large as the British
Isles, or with such a relatively fertile and extensive lowland
plain (stretching to the Pennines and Scottish Lowlands in
the North and the Welsh mountains in the West), and
capable of supporting a large population. Sea power, an
island base, and a strong, unified state gave Britain a
strategic mobility, a flexibility, and a security which land-
based powers lacked. Britain could afford to develop an
oceanic strategy aimed at domination of the world economy, whilst other states were forced into continental
entanglements.[9]

From 1650 onwards the British state began to pursue an
outward-looking policy designed to assist the efforts of its
merchants and its settlers in the struggle for the New
World. The policy was never formalised as a doctrine and
was not always pursued consistently. It was particularly
vulnerable to the shifting balance of power between
interests and factions in the English Parliament. Neverthe-
less the new course marked out in the few short years of the
English republic after the execution of the King endured. It
was a policy which increasingly put British commercial
interests first and subordinated other considerations to
them. Under Cromwell the Navigation Acts were passed,
and these created a single national monopoly for British
trade, open to all British merchants to engage in. The
majority of the old trading monopolies were abolished; all
trade had henceforward to be carried in British ships, and
all the existing colonies were brought directly under the
control of Parliament. Trade wars were fought with the
Dutch and the Spanish, the Dutch monopoly of trade was
broken, Jamaica seized, and an important alliance concluded with Portugal gave access to the Portuguese colonial
empire in return for British naval protection. This new
aggressive policy was continued after the Restoration,
although without much success at first. All the wars of the
next 150 years had a commercial purpose.[10] Britain fought
Holland, Spain and France for control of the world
economy, the possession of the new territories and mastery
of the sea.

The colonial system, practised by all states, treated colonies as foreign estates, tended by settlers or by slaves, and designed to add directly to the wealth and importance of the home country. Taxation of them was often heavy, and their trade was strictly controlled, while the emigration to them of surplus labour was encouraged. Each nation tried to insist that its own traders should enjoy a monopoly of trade in its own colonies. This was why wars were so frequent.

Britain eventually emerged as the overwhelming victor in this struggle, and acquired in the course of it a potent definition of its national interest and a coherent strategic doctrine. Enunciated most clearly by leaders like William Pitt, its basic principles were simple. Britain should concentrate on its navy, maintaining only small land forces. British governments should avoid entanglements on the continent of Europe, and where these proved unavoidable the British aim should be to aid its allies with money rather than with armies. The major British military effort was to be concentrated at sea, securing the safety of the British Isles and prosecuting war in the New World. Britain's allies in Europe frequently found themselves bearing the brunt of the European war, whilst Britain devoted her energies to securing yet more overseas territory and agreeing peace terms when the objectives had been secured. This caused some resentment; Frederick the Great denounced Britain as 'perfidious Albion'. British policy became known for its ruthlessness, its single mindedness and its occasional treachery and hypocrisy. But there was no doubting its success. France, although a wealthier and more populous nation than Britain, was comprehensively defeated during the eighteenth century in the battle for the New World, losing both India and Canada, and was stalemated in Europe by the alliance of continental powers which Britain organised against her.

The Napoleonic wars were the last of the great colonial wars of the seventeenth and eighteenth centuries. The basic reason for Napoleon's defeat was that during the whole war France fought on two fronts — in Europe and throughout the world — whereas the British, until the final stages, fought only on one. Unable to break the stranglehold of British sea power, or to damage British trade with Europe, Napoleon finally succumbed to the coalition of absolute Monarchs which Britain had organised against him. Britain entered the war on the side of European Reaction and against the Revolution, because a Revolutionary France, no less than an Absolutist France, challenged the commercial and strategic interests of the British state. Napoleon's defeat spelt the end of the French challenge for European and world hegemony, leaving Britain with the bulk of the spoils.

The only great setback to this policy up to 1815 was the successful rebellion of the American colonies in 1783 – the most important of Britain's overseas possessions. The burden of taxes and controls the British attempted to maintain on the American states eventually drove the colonists into revolt. The loss was a major one, and the eventual consequences for Britain were momentous, but at the time it did not stop Britain's advance to world power. The system of colonies and protected commerce, the trade in slaves and sugar, the looting of India, which had so augmented British strength and wealth in the eighteenth century, were rapidly overtaken in the early nineteenth century by a new source of power – modern industry.

2.3   Industrialisation and free trade

The great spurt of British industrialisation, which took place after 1780 and continued during the Napoleonic wars, meant that by 1815 Britain no longer dominated the world economy only through its navy, its extensive colonies, and its protected trade, but also through the much greater productivity of its leading industries. A major change in British strategy and policy was to follow. The colonial and commercial imperialism of the previous 250 years was to take second place to a new imperialism of free trade. The debate which raged in Britain in the early nineteenth century was not about whether Britain should have an empire or not, nor whether Britain should aspire to world power or not, but whether that empire should be based primarily on a free trade open to all the world, or on a protected trade based on the colonies. The argument that was put forward by all the interests and groups supporting free trade was that free trade was the cheapest policy to secure Britain's continuing domination of the world economy. The lead in productivity and technology which British industries had established meant that if trade was open, British goods had a decisive competitive advantage. They could undersell any rivals in price and out-perform them in quality. As one supporter of free trade expressed it during the debate in Parliament on the bill to repeal the Corn Laws, free trade was the beneficent principle by which 'foreign nations would become valuable colonies to us, without imposing on us the responsibility of governing them'.[11]

The strategy that had generally predominated since 1650 was a shrewd commercial policy, which exploited the opportunities that came Britain's way and made full use of the geographical and political advantages Britain enjoyed. The dispute over whether to adopt a policy of complete free trade in the decades after 1815 was a sharp one, because the position of a major domestic interest – the landowners and their tenant farmers – had necessarily to be sacrificed if the protection of agriculture was to be ended. But repeal when it came was only the last stage in a lengthy process of adjustment. Successive administrations since the 1820s had been reducing duties and opening British markets, because commercial interest now dictated it so strongly. There was no domestic lobby arguing for complete protection – the whole of the property-owning class had benefited too much from trade and the colonial system. The substance of the debate was over the question of the balance between agriculture and commerce. Those political economists, like Malthus, who argued the landowners' case, claimed that it was folly to risk destroying the agricultural base of society to realise what might prove only a temporary advantage in commerce.

The supporters of the Corn Laws were defeated because the balance of social forces had already shifted decisively against them. The importance of commerce and expansion abroad and the extent of industrialisation at home ensured the isolation of the protectionists. The new and rapidly expanding urban working class supported the relaxing of the Corn Laws in the hope of cheaper food. Fear of social disorder was used by the free traders as the final circumstance to clinch the case for repeal, but the central argument for it lay in their overwhelming confidence that complete free trade was the best means of extending and consolidating Britain's wealth and power in the world economy.[12]

The relative ease with which the transition to free trade was made is what now seems remarkable. The extent of the shift that was occurring was not fully realised either then or for long afterwards, because it seemed so in line with the traditional principle of maximising commercial advantage that had guided British expansion. Yet the move to free trade proved one of the decisive events of modern British history, perhaps *the* decisive event. Britain had participated in the world economy and had profited greatly from its growing network of trade, but always from a position of self-sufficiency. It did not depend on the world economy for its survival. The industrial and technological lead which Britain had established by 1850, and the naval strength and colonial possessions which already made Britain the leading power in the world economy, persuaded Britain's leaders that the abandonment of self-sufficiency and protection was not reckless, but the way to preserve British power in the future. Britain became the first major state to become dependent for the regular supplies of food and raw materials necessary to sustain its population on a trading link with areas of the world economy, over which Britain could not necessarily exercise control.

Since 1850 Britain's position in the world economy has been precarious and vulnerable. This was disguised at first, partly because British power and wealth continued to increase, partly because British agriculture was not immediately affected in the way that had been feared. But the final result was not altered. Britain's future and very survival became tied to the world economy. Free trade assisted the tremendous growth of the population to a size far beyond any level that could be supported by food production in

Britain.[13] Imports of food and raw materials raised foreign incomes, encouraged economic development, and so expanded markets for British manufactured goods and services. A new world division of labour sprang up with Britain at its centre, specialising as the world's workshop and exchanging its manufactures, particularly cotton goods and iron and steel, for the primary products of the rest of the world.[14]

2.4 The beginnings of decline

It could not last. For a time it brought Britain unparalleled dominance and wealth. But the very success of British industrialisation and the policy of free trade created the first great world capitalist boom during the 1850s and 1860s. Aided by exports of capital and machine tools from Britain, several other states began to industrialise extremely rapidly. The communications, the financial network, the trading system of the world economy were all developed enormously and all came to centre on London. This further increased the importance and the influence of Britain and permitted the further expansion of the businesses of the City to service the whole of the world economy. They came to supply a great part of its financial, shipping and insurance needs.

The industrialisation of the world economy, and the resulting development of the accumulation of capital on a world scale, meant that the predominance of British naval and commercial power came under threat. Whilst Britain might still use its naval power in the traditional manner to force states like China to open themselves to the penetration of British capital and British goods,[15] and to safeguard the trade arteries of the world economy, there was no way of similarly compelling the new industrial states like Germany and the United States to maintain free trade. To protect themselves from British competition, every strong nation-state seeking to industrialise protected its industries with high tariffs, designed to shut out British goods, whilst denouncing free trade as a hypocritical policy designed to promote British industry at the expense of the rest of the world.[16]

By the 1880s a new balance of power was already emerging in the world economy, and Britain's capacity to remain its leading state and the guarantor of the conditions world-wide under which accumulation of capital could proceed became more and more precarious. British decline begins with the rise of modern industry on a truly world scale. The challenge posed to Britain by Germany and the United States was both commercial and military, and it brought forth a new debate about Britain's foreign economic policy and its role in the world, the first of many during the hundred years decline. The tariff reformers[17] began to question whether free trade was still in Britain's commercial and strategic interest. They argued that it was now involving such costs that, just as the protectionism of the old colonial system had been abandoned for free trade, so now a further shift in policy had become necessary if the fruits of British expansion were to be preserved. There developed the great controversy over free trade and tariff reform which dominated discussion of economic policy in the early years of the century. But it was never simply a narrow debate about the best commercial policy for Britain. It ranged far wider, to focus upon the nature of Britain's Empire and world leadership and how they could best be preserved and decline averted.

The imperialism of the tariff reformers was a new perspective and a new programme, because the loss of the American colonies, the steady advance of free trade, and the informal empire it had created, persuaded most political leaders by the middle of the nineteenth century that the colonies were no longer an asset but a drain on the metropolitan country. 'Millstones around our necks' was Disraeli's judgement, and it summed up a widely held view even amongst those (like Disraeli himself) who opposed repeal of the Corn Laws. The radical wing of Liberalism, which included Richard Cobden and John Bright, went much further in condemning colonies, not only as very costly in taxes, but also as a means of perpetuating national rivalries and wars between nations. Free trade was held to promote cosmopolitanism and mutual interdependence, so undermining nation-states and promoting world peace.[18]

Despite considerable anti-colonial settlement, no British government parted with any British colony, and by the last two decades of the nineteenth century the colonial empire was appearing in a new light. The drive to industrialise had reawakened national rivalry and competition among nation-states for control of the world economy that Britain policed and serviced. A scramble for control of what territory still lay outside European control began, particularly for the inland areas of Africa. Britain, still possessing superior naval power and an unrivalled network of military bases and client states, was in a position to take the greater part of the spoils, and did so. Free trade and imperialism were reconciled in a new aggressive policy. An age of imperial expansion began, which was accompanied by mounting imperialist frenzy in all the major capitalist states. Britain's new insecurity and growing militarism and Jingoism[19] arose because the world seemed suddenly filled with industrial powers, whose metropolitan bases in terms of resources and manpower and industrial production were potentially much more powerful than Britain's. Trade rivalry and military rivalry became fused into one. To the tariff reform movement it seemed obvious that Britain could only remain a world power in the changed circumstances of the world economy by organising its world empire more effectively and revitalising its industry. As the centre of an Empire that covered one-fifth of the earth's surface Britain could secure its vital interests, particularly the supplies of food and raw materials for its metropolitan population and industries. But the actual empire that existed was chaotic. Much of it had been inherited from the pre-industrial colonial system, including the major territory under British rule, India. Much of the rest, particularly the territories in Africa, had not been acquired because of any kind of plan or systematic economic logic, but as a response to initiatives taken independently to British settlers, traders, and adventurers, or to forestall involvement by foreign powers.[20]

The tariff reformers drew on earlier ideas for transforming the Empire into an Anglo-Saxon world empire. The overseas expansion of the Anglo-Saxon race offered an opportunity for the creation of a truly effective and united Empire.[21] Colonies that were merely administered and held down by the metropolitan power were costly, but colonies that were settled by British subjects could become communities linked directly to Britain and could add significantly to British strength. What the tariff reform movement wanted was to construct an Anglo-Saxon empire in which Anglo-Saxon culture, Anglo-Saxon institutions, and Anglo-Saxon capital would predominate. Where this was clearly impossible, as in India and some of the African territories, the ideology of the 'white man's burden' suggested a paternalistic administration of the territories to raise them to civilisation. But the real desire of the tariff reformers was to create an imperial federation, which could be as united as Britain itself.[22]

The policy did not ultimately succeed. The principal settler colonies – Canada, Australia, New Zealand, South Africa – made it plain that they wanted independence, not federation,[23] whilst at home the policy of tariff reform was consigned to ineffective though vocal opposition with the election of a Liberal government, unequivocally committed to free trade, in 1906, which stayed in office until after the outbreak of war in 1914.[24]

One of the most remarkable aspects of British policy in the last eighty years has been this dogged commitment to free trade. The rival economic programme of the tariff reformers was only seriously attempted twice – briefly during the First World War, and then after 1931 when the world trading and financial order had broken down. By the 1950s it was clear that the tariff reformers' dream was over. They had failed to shift British policy on to a new course and free trade again became dominant.

The dilemma that faced the British state was acute. As a result of the formal and informal empires which British expansion had created, Britain derived some economic benefit from its colonies, but still greater benefit from being the financial and commercial centre of the capitalist world economy.[25] British manufacturing industry might be challenged and overtaken in some areas, but the international monetary system was centred on sterling and the international trade system on London. Apart from the complex shipping, insurance and banking services which were now provided for the world economy from London, Britain benefited enormously from the free flow of goods and food. Since the agricultural interest had been defeated, the dumping of cheap food on British markets was welcomed on all sides. The fact that the programme of tariff reform would have raised food prices was one of the main reasons why working-class opinion swung against it. From the standpoint of British capital, a further advantage from the world economy was the scope for British investment abroad. Assets reached the enormous total of £4000 million in 1914, which meant a steady investment income of some £200 million a year for British rentiers.[26]

A decision to abandon the effort to maintain the free flow of goods and capital, and instead to launch a bid to establish a new protectionist and self-sufficient bloc within the world economy, risked the stability of the world economy and went against the principle of maximising commercial opportunities for its subjects, which had so long guided British policy. The British had long regarded themselves as the most enlightened nation in the world economy, because they were willing to bear some of the burdens of maintaining the conditions for a free movement of goods, capital, and labour in the world economy, which was so greatly improving the wealth and speeding the development of all the separate nation-states participating in it. The continued possession of a formal Empire by Britain was widely viewed as an unfortunate necessity, a means of ensuring British predominance and allowing Britain to discharge its traditional world role. As Halford Mackinder put it:

> Under a condition of universal free trade, the dream of the sixties of the last century, industrial life and empire might be dissociated, but when competing industries seek to monopolise markets by means of customs tariffs, even democracies are compelled to annexe empires. In the last two generations . . . the object of vast British annexations has been to support a trade open to all the world.[27]

Accompanying this traditional policy of free trade imperialism there had evolved a military doctrine, which was
distilled in the nineteenth century into the strategic
principles that the ocean highways must be kept open and
the continent of Europe must be kept divided. The first
meant the maintenance of a strong navy to a two power
standard;[28] the second meant that, at the very least, no
hostile power should be allowed to become so predominant
in Europe that it could control Belgium and Holland. Some
British strategists became obsessed with the duel for world
domination between sea power and land power, and argued
that it was a fundamental British interest that no power
should arise or win control of the heartland of the Eurasian
continent, where its base would be secure from attack by
sea, and from which it could put pressure on the world's
coasts and ports which Britain dominated, and ultimately
raise a naval force to challenge Britain.[29]

Britain fought major wars to prevent first France, then
Germany, rising to a position of supremacy within Europe
and threatening Britain's world empire and the security of
its island base. But whereas Britain emerged from the
Napoleonic wars as the undisputed power in the world
economy, and embarked on a century of world domination
and leadership, Britain emerged from the First World War
only nominally victorious. The price of defeating Germany
was the alliance with the United States. Britain was proved
to be no longer militarily or industrially strong enough to
maintain itself as the dominant world power. The rise of the
United States signalled the eclipse of Britain's traditional
role.[30]

2.5   Britain and the world economy

The course of the hundred years decline was shaped
decisively by two momentous choices. The first was the
continued adherence to free trade and to the institutions of
the liberal world order long after the conditions which had
originally recommended it had disappeared. The second
was the decision to fight Germany rather than the United